ALL SOUL PARTS RETURNED

All Soul Parts Returned

Poems by

Bruce Beasley

American Poets Continuum Series, No. 163

BOA Editions, Ltd.   Rochester, NY   2017

First Edition
17 18 19 20 7 6 5 4 3 2 1

For information about permission to reuse any material from this book, please contact The Permissions Company at www.permissionscompany.com or e-mail permdude@gmail.com.

Publications by BOA Editions, Ltd.—a not-for-profit corporation under section 501 (c) (3) of the United States Internal Revenue Code—are made possible with funds from a variety of sources, including public funds from the Literature Program of the National Endowment for the Arts; the New York State Council on the Arts, a state agency; and the County of Monroe, NY. Private funding sources include the Lannan Foundation for support of the Lannan Translations Selection Series; the Max and Marian Farash Charitable Foundation; the Mary S. Mulligan Charitable Trust; the Rochester Area Community Foundation; the Steeple-Jack Fund; the Ames-Amzalak Memorial Trust in memory of Henry Ames, Semon Amzalak, and Dan Amzalak; and contributions from many individuals nationwide. See Colophon on page 128 for special individual acknowledgments.

ART WORKS.
arts.gov

State of the Arts

NYSCA

Cover Art: Artwork by J. B. Murray courtesy of the J. B. Murray Estate
Cover Design: Sandy Knight
Interior Design and Composition: Richard Foerster
BOA Logo: Mirko

Library of Congress Cataloging-in-Publication Data

Names: Beasley, Bruce, 1958– author.
Title: All soul parts returned : poems / by Bruce Beasley.
Description: First edition. | Rochester, NY : BOA Editions Ltd., 2017. |
  Series: American poets continuum ; no. 163
Identifiers: LCCN 2017018009 (print) | LCCN 2017024101 (ebook) | ISBN
  9781942683469 (eBook) | ISBN 9781942683452
Subjects: | BISAC: POETRY / Inspirational & Religious. | RELIGION /
  Christianity / Catholic. | RELIGION / Mysticism. | BODY, MIND & SPIRIT /
  Spirituality / Shamanism.
Classification: LCC PS3552.E1748 (ebook) | LCC PS3552.E1748 A6 2017 (print) |
  DDC 811/.54—dc23
LC record available at https://lccn.loc.gov/2017018009

BOA Editions, Ltd.
250 North Goodman Street, Suite 306
Rochester, NY 14607
www.boaeditions.org
A. Poulin, Jr., Founder (1938–1996)

for Suzanne and Jin
souls of all my soul parts

THE PARTS

Torn-to-Pieces-Hood
9

Part I *Thou Must Leave*

Report to the Provost on the Progress of My Leave   21
Me Meaneth   25
Reading Jesus Again, with a New Prescription   31

Part II *Disorientation Psalm for Schopenhauer*

Tohu Bohu   39
Looking Down the Cliff, with Schopenhauer, on Black Friday   43
The Last Good   46
"I Don't Like My Soul Parts"   48
Reading *The Purpose Driven Life*, with Schopenhauer   49

Part III *Hymeneal*

Nuptial Song   57
On Marriage   61
Antithalamion   63
What Do You Think the Poet Is Trying to Say?   67
The Name of the Island Was Marriage   70
Offspring Insprung   74

Part IV *The Sixth Dust*

Revised Catechism   81
Cleft for Me Let Me Hide Myself from Thee   83
Such and Such and Such and Such   85

Part V *The Mass of the Ordinary*

Kyrie	93
Embolism	95
Sanctus	98
Credo	100
Fraction Rite	102
Agnus Dei	106
Benedictus	109
Gloria	112

NONORDINARY TO THE POEMS	115

Acknowledgments	*121*
About the Author	*123*
Colophon	*128*

Torn-to-Pieces-Hood

Come undone, soul. It's what you've wanted, isn't it, to go to pieces. Dismember, scatter self from Self.

Who knew the soul had frequently been torn? Had shed its parts all over and they'd fled to hide, piece by piece, in a murky otherworld known only as Nonordinary Reality.

So say the shamans. So say the shamans who offer for a fee to bring them back, in a drum-drone and trance and stench of incense, to trace the hollows, sky-fissures, lower and upper realms of the Nonordinary and cajole those cowering fragments back to a mass of their kin soul parts, here in the Ordinary. To breathe them back onto forehead and chest, brain and heart. Who is *I* but the mass of its soul parts, the ones that stayed, the ones that—like the gospel's prodigal son—left and squandered and came back, ready even to eat the slop of the swine?

"The constitutional disease from which I suffer," William James wrote in a letter, "is what the Germans call *Zerrissenheit* or torn-to-pieces-hood."

A *mass* is a collection of incoherent parts seen nevertheless as a singular entirety. A mass of errors. Torn-to-pieces-hood as a mass of rent remainders that populate, all unknowingly, the ordinary.

Ordinary means, among its mass of other meanings, "commonplace, unexceptional, of no particular interest or importance." *Ordinary* means, among its mass of other meanings, the collection of chants and prayers that form the body of the Roman Catholic Mass. In the Ordinary of the Mass the god-who-came-back enters, again and again, the wafer and the wine, enters again and again into Time, into Ordinary Reality, to reheal all over again our latest state of torn-to-pieces-hood.

When the traumatized soul-in-pieces flees Ordinary Reality, it leaves, too, the Ordinary of the Mass, tears apart the fabric of the mass of the ordinary.

On this, as on every, point, the Baltimore Catechism is quite without doubt: "A spirit is also indivisible; it cannot be divided into parts."

Parts of us are always leaving. More and more stray soul pieces crowd the Nonordinary. So much can pull the soul apart, like rain slashing through a spiderweb strand. Any part can find it easier to make its way on its own in the Nonordinary, when it's terrified, bereaved, rejected, in despair. "Most of us in Western culture have been walking around for some period of time without parts of our soul," says a shamanist website, matter-of-factly. All these tatters where soul once was, like a worm-eaten book.

"Human life must be some kind of mistake," wrote Arthur Schopenhauer, who must have left a vapor trail of soul parts behind him everywhere he went.

"If you imagine . . . the sum total of distress, pain, and suffering of every kind which the sun shines upon in its course," he wrote, "you will have to admit it would have been much better if the sun had been able to call up the phenomenon of life as little on earth as on the moon."

Soul parts, once the shaman has hauled them back, "won't put up with any shenanigans," says a shamanist's pamphlet. "If you do nothing with the soul parts, they could go into repeat soul loss . . . leaving you feeling worse than before the soul retrieval."

No soul has time for *shenanigans*. It is busy rending its garments, like a desert prophet.

I think a part of my soul is coming back. Last night I dreamed my father, who died when I was fifteen, had never made it all the way into his grave, though my twin brother and I had hauled his corpse there ourselves, dragging it upright between us through the woods. My sister said she kept seeing him out of the corner of her eye, and once, she told me, on an unlit road he had reached into her car, running beside it, grabbing the steering wheel while she tried to hit the accelerator hard enough to lose him. He's still out there, she told me. He's coming back.

Forgive my soul parts; they know not what they do.

Even St. Augustine knew the soul could get dislodged. He punned on the Latin for *religion*, which meant to re-tie, to re-bind, like a ligament. "True religion is that by which the soul is united to God so that it binds itself again [*religat*] by reconciliation to him from whom it had broken off."

"Faith," says Calvin, "is tossed about by various doubts, so that the minds of the godly are rarely at peace."

In the Mass the Eucharist is called the "unbloody sacrifice." It reenacts the crucifixion, sacrifices again and again the god from whom we have broken off. We're spared—except for what in the "goodly chalice" is blood but doesn't taste like it—the gore of that offering. Could the giving-away of our soul parts be, itself, an "unbloody sacrifice"? An oblation, an offertory? Giving back to God the parts of ourselves He gave us, like manna, desert-rain.

O Lord, accept this offering into Your hands.

Down the body of the catechism runs a ligament, fibrous tissue that connects startled question to rote-memorizable answer. It's no soul; it won't tear easily.

Q. How is the soul like to God?
A. The soul is like to God because it is a spirit that will never die.

Q. What do the words "will never die" mean?
A. By the words "will never die" we mean that the soul, when once created, will never cease to exist, whatever be its condition in the next world.

Q. Why then do we say a soul is dead while in a state of mortal sin?
A. We say a soul is dead while in a state of mortal sin, because in that state it is as helpless as a dead body, and can merit nothing for itself.

So Despair can kill what cannot die. Despair's a mortal sin, one that makes the soul rejoice, ironically, in its own mortality. It's the soul in pieces, its torn-off remnants huddled in the Nonordinary, praying no shaman ever comes to find them there.

When the gods go to war against each other—like the chaos gods and the creation gods almost always do In the Beginning—it's called a *theomachy*. A civil war inside the soul I call an *automachy*. Between the soul parts that despair and want out and others that stay, still hoping human life might not be, after all, just some mistake.

"Why art thou sad, O my soul," asks the Psalm, "and why art thou disquieted against me?"

"Only say the word," says the Mass's Ordinary, "and my soul shall be healed."

Q. What do the words "and my soul shall be healed" mean?

The soul missing some of its parts feels un-at-home in the universe. Deadened, debilitated. Torn-to-pieces-hood tears the soul even more to pieces. If one soul part is restored, a shaman tells me, often the others begin to return on their own like, she says, pearls on a necklace.

The pearl of great price. Sell everything you own in order to possess it.

"Soul, don't take offense," pleads Szymborska, "that I've only got you now and then."

To become a shaman, a shaman tells me, you must become utterly dismembered. Sometimes your own spirit animal will turn on you, rend you into pieces.

Hegel knew *Zerrissenheit*. "The life of the spirit," he wrote, "is not the life that shrinks from death and keeps itself untouched by devastation, but rather the life that endures it and maintains itself in it. It wins its truth only when, in *der absoluten Zerrissenheit* [utter torn-to-pieces-hood; absolute dismemberment] it finds itself."

Q. What do the words "it finds itself" mean?

Come, Holy Spirit. One-who-heals. Dismemberer. Come, undoer, undone.

FREQUENTLY ASKED QUESTIONS

People ask the same questions in the days, weeks, and months that follow their soul retrievals.

Q. *My soul parts don't like me.*
A. Of course they don't (but it's good that you know how they feel). First we betrayed them by sending them away. Then we forgot them and left them there. And now that they are back they discover that we are boring.

Q. *I don't like my soul parts.*
A. So now you have an intimate understanding of why they left. Wouldn't you leave if people didn't like you? . . . Every soul part contains a gift or talent. What do you need to heal in your relationship with yourself to gain access to that treasure?

—Last Mask Center for Shamanic Healing

Augustine: Then, since a word consists of sound and meaning, and the sound has to do with the ears and the meaning with the mind, do you not think that in a word, just as in some living being, the sound is the body and the meaning is, as it were, the soul?

Evodius: To me the similarity is most striking.

Augustine: . . . But when the dismemberment of the sound into its letters results in the loss of its meaning, you do not suppose, do you, that anything else has occurred than the departure of the soul from a torn body? . . .

—St. Augustine, *The Measure of the Soul*

NONORDINARY TO THE POEMS on page 115 contains notes, definitions, and other departed parts of many of the poems.

PART I
THOU MUST LEAVE

REPORT TO THE PROVOST ON THE PROGRESS OF MY LEAVE

In me thou see'st the glowing of such fire,
That on the ashes of his youth doth lie,
As the deathbed whereon it must expire

—Shakespeare, Sonnet 73

*

I have taken, with your blessing, leave
of several of my senses,

let them slip without a tug from what has often choked them
then dragged the empty collars by their leashes, spikes
clattering all morning and afternoon down the leafblocked yellow streets.

* *

I've gone missing,

the way someone else
might go drinking, caroling.
I have gone

from house to house, missing, gathering
back the parts of parts of me I've left

self-strewn behind. But already again
I find myself
a stranger and sojourner among all these

my catalogued and dissilient pieces.

* * *

Left
fallow, I shall be

sown no more, nor
pruned. Only these

hard-cracked, weed-
choked rows of stubble.

* * * *

I would as soon
self-yield, as when,
half-gone in nitrous oxide, I saw my self—
with its spit-suction cup and plaque-scratchings—

beneath myself

as one wholly arbitrary site to locate such a long
history of doing, thinking, having-done.
A few feet of flesh, merely mammalian, mind
frost-misting around it, a life

I could either take or, more likely, leave,
and the hygienist suspected something going
strange and said, giving
that patient's shoulder a tiny, intimate shake,

I'm here. I'm still here.

* * * * *

Or was that me
speaking?
There lay some body, with its little paper bib.

Of the ultimate things, says Dickinson, *Parting—is all we know.*

* * * * * *

Everything, of late, seems
of late,

steeped in its too-lateness.
Almost everything surpasseth understanding.

Some scintillation glimpsed from the last things
  ashes   *youth*
  deathbed *expire* some
intermurmuring music I can sometimes make out

  bare *ruined*
  fadeth late something
far away and intimate that sings

of what is last, all-lasting, nearly here.
Since I have gone absconditus the odds

have evened I can hear it   *thou must leave*
let it rise through the ruined

choirs of my ears
and take it in.

To leave means *not* to take.
But I will take

your part, unknowable To-Come.
I will take every last bit of it.

       * * * * * * *

As required I have sealed up all
in rest. Desisted
from all duties and exertions,

deserted. The way
the lilies of the field, which
neither toil nor spin, still split

and split their bulbs
underearth. Per the terms
of my original proposal,

my soul hath cloven, and murmured strangely. Self-
sabbathing, I have learned
to leave that well

which I *must* love, again and again, ere long.

Me Meaneth

I.

The calf lay meaning herself.
What does that *mean?* The calf
lay moaning in the pasture. As

in a long-forgotten Scottish poet's lines
the dictionary lets demonstrate
one thing *mean*

once meant: to moan, to lament—
The speaned lambs mene their mithers
As they wimple ower the bent.

I can't stop myself from muttering that, though you're
annoyed: What's *speaned?* what's *mene?* what's *mither?* what's
wimple? what's *bent?*

We could trace it if we wanted to: the dictionary's
words line up like children in a rush,
blindfolded, to bash

a piñata. We could track
T. S. Cairncross himself,
and his lost poem, and his lambs,

the words that merge
into his last name—
but what would that heap

of memory-stones commemorate?
The cairns lay along the crossroads. The calf lay meaning
in the fields. The speaned lambs wimple as they mean.

What's *mither*? —Mother. What's *ower*? —Over. What's *bent*?
—A grass of a reedy or rush-like habit.
But what's *rush-like*? What's a *habit*?

The lallation of rushes, over the slough.
Scythe-pass after lamb-spean, and the sick
calf meaning herself

there, gnat-rush
from her rheumed eyes
with each slow blink.

For *speaned*
read *weaned. Wimple*'s
the cloth folds across the face

in a nun's habit, or the analogous
pleats on a body of water.
The slough wind-wimples

as its gnats lift in wave on wave.
To wimple is to veil, or to fall
in folds, or

(what Cairncross must have had
in the folds of his mind) to walk
unsteadily, shiftily, like the newborn

lambs staggering after their mother,
weaned too soon, meaning
the withheld warmth of milk-spurt.

So *moan* and *mean* burst
from the same rush
and word-thatch, the same

bent bent. *The weaned lambs*
moan for their mothers, we could say,
as they stagger over dry grass. But I like the way

Cairncross made the words
wimple, the deep
infolds and shadow-pools of them.

I'm still unspeaned
from vowel, consonant-smear on white-sopped lips.
Let the words mean wrong, in the mouthfeel of their moan.

II.

When *me meaneth* meant
it grieves me, English knew
something it's forgotten: how, reflexive,

our denotations come back at us, and it hurts,
to be the only one who *can* possess
your own intention. You won't know what I mean by that.

You keep saying, *You see what I'm saying?*
but it's only speech-punctuation, like *like,* like
Know what I mean?, by which you mean

to celebrate the significative
interpenetration of your desire
to speak, and mine to listen, and in listening hear exactly as you mean.

III.

Meaning was said
to be there, *especially* there, on that façade, but we
could get nowhere near it:
the scaffolds and platforms, workboots and drills, all the

machinery of restoration interfering.
We stood staring at the sun-stab off aluminum,
the blowtorch-blast and jackhammerer's
sweatglint down the neck

as if they *were*
the storied edifice they concealed:
some bas relief Last Judgment's
hellbound bodywrithe just behind

the metal lunch pail's dried and dented
tomato stains shivering with that offcast light.

IV.

She meaned as to the state of her soul, wrote a preacher.
My gret unease full oft I meanne, says Chaucer.
Think not that thou art sufficiently mortified—
some dyspeptic poet I've never
heard of had to say—
And speanéd from the world.

Mean means
poor but *having means* means rich.

I have the means
the way I have the blues.

As if a meantime like now
were a time
all seething with signification: so much you couldn't hold it in your mind.

V.

The gists
of things sometimes go

out, like the wireless
connection when the hamsters yanked

the router's wires through their bars
and frayed them in a tangle of red-into-green
throughout their sopped nest,
and elsewhere the hourglass icon

kept spilling its sand across the screen.

So sometimes what's meant by God

goes out,
goes out.

VI.

I mean my mother: I can hear her
labored, final breathing I never heard, as I step
on this sticktangle by traintracks

(are they *bents*?),
their static-crack like Styrofoam underfoot.
They sound like trapped air, the way her lungs

filled and shut themselves
overnight when she was fifty, and I was gone.
My brother breathed for her awhile.

She's senseless now, as in nothing
available anymore to her fivefold senses.
She's meaningless, as in

impervious to any further meanings, as
in incapable of grieving ever again.
She's obsolete

and present
as the verb
I use to grieve her:

to moan, to mourn, to *mean*. Speaned
from this world, sufficiently
mortified.

The speaned man
menes his mither
as he wimples
ower the bent.

Reading Jesus Again, with a New Prescription

Whoever wants to save his life will lose it.
—The Complete Jesus

There will be days, I'm told You said, *when you will not see me.*
It's one of those days.

It's one of those days, Winebibber,
Glutton, Consorter-with-Whores, when verily
I can hear You, no
translation needed: *Thou*
art lukewarm, I will
spew thee out of my mouth.

I have listened to each of Your prescriptions, reread
every scripture that attributes any utterance to You.
The Kingdom of Heaven is at hand: everyone agrees
You said that, if nothing else.

My hands keep snatching at air.
Before Abraham was, I am, You said. And still *are:*
I hope You are.

I *want* to save
this life, Lord, or
lose it

so turn

again toward You. Eyesalve
rubbed under my lids, to see You well.
Will You come to me, straight from Your Father, trailing
scourges, nails, grails of vinegar and gall, all
the paraphernalia of Your wounding, Your
taking-this-life.

Woe to you who stand in need of grace
(did You really say that?)—

I so stand, Cosmocrator.

Is, and Was, and Is-to-Come, when will You
come near. Come
on like these side-effects that—
like emaciated John the Baptist
with his fur-robe-rags and chipped-gold
script-wrapped crook—prepare the way:
hypersomnolence, insomnia, "abnormal"
dreams, anxiety, agitation, suicidal fixation,
hostility, inability to sit still.

"This is not a complete list
of all side effects that may occur.
If they are bothersome,
check with your doctor."

Lord, Lord, Your hour,
You proclaimed, is coming, and now

was. Has come, indeed, and now is

as though it never were.

I barely sleep now, so have
no abnormal dreams.
This, to me, is *bothersome*, Lord.

Release the Time.

I lie striped in lightslats from the garbage alley
struck across the bed,
4 a.m., thinking

of what vast neuronal net
must Yours be, what
abnormalities of likeness-making in Your dreaming,
what hostility and inability to sit still, what
recriminations and self-loathings and
dreads-at-having-done

as, for instance, having
put us to life on this earth: do Your night-thoughts still
perseverate on that?

———————————

Like You I have wanted to put off
this body of flesh;
I have tried to put
off—short-circuit—these neuronal nets
of hebetude and death's
nothing-loath. Put on the light

like the overhead in my bedroom
that sputters and extinguishes
till I slam the loose-wired wall switch,
squeeze it for a long time sealed Up.

———————————

Did You say—or did I dream
it (I've been dreaming again, abnormally,
of You): *Why do you say Lord, Lord,
and still not follow Me?*

———————————

I've been doing what You told me not to: praying
with vain repetition.
Amen, amen, amen, amen, amen, amen,
many of my supplications go:
terminus without genesis, Apocalypse
with no Torah.

I see everywhere the dead
burying their own dead, even me.
I would drop
my gravedirt-clumped boots and follow You.

But, ineffable Who Is, which
Via Crucis did You take (they branch
in every direction I can see)?

———————————————

Neurocrator,
forget the writing, the riddling: leap
from neuron to neuron, a trillion
times every split second.
There are forty quadrillion synaptic connections to be tried
in my brain alone. Trigger
each axon, each dendrite, and come
again here, Jesus, neuro-
parousial:
there's Cosmos enough for You in this skull, there's
plenty Chaos enough.

———————————————

Most winters my soul starts
dwindling again, shedding its pieces
around Christmas, dim solstice, incarnation
of the lightless

death-likeness.

Mind's eschaton, old-year's Tenebrae.

Brain like a whited sepulcher,
corrupted-
down-into-purity
bones of loathing.

Wyeth Labs has a cure for that now.
Why do you not follow me.
The latest covenant comes,
time-releasable, in three
daily tablets.
I take them, and eat; do
this, in full memorium of You.

He who does not
hate his soul
cannot follow Me: can I
still follow You?

PART II
DISORIENTATION PSALM
FOR SCHOPENHAUER

. . . the truth that we have not to rejoice but rather to mourn at the existence
of the world; —that its nonexistence would be preferable
to its existence; that it is something which at bottom ought not to be;
&c., &c.

—Arthur Schopenhauer

Tohu Bohu

&c. _____ &c.

Life is good.
___ Strongly disagree
___ Moderately disagree
___ Slightly disagree
___ Slightly agree
___ Moderately agree
___ Strongly agree

The Oxford Happiness Questionnaire

Here among your barbed et ceteras, next week's Thanksgiving
and I've been reading, of all things, you,
who couldn't give thanks if your guts depended on it.

The sky today is downright Schopenhauerian:

dim and glum, light-sucked,
as if its purpose were to obfuscate the revealed.

Write with me a Psalm of Disorientation, Schopenhauer.
It annoyed you that God declared things good:
His compulsive ordering and self-congratulation,

His *fiat lux.* You stayed stuck in the *tohu bohu*, the waste-and-void.
Like a chaos god, you'd have left us all there,
starved—without even being able to know it—of Being.

Still, there's praise to be had, and we'll huddle
around its whitecrumble of coals,
rub and puff at our hands,

give our skin-friction and lung-warmth
back to ourselves
as if from some beneficent somewhere-else.

&c. _____ &c.

Wretched, miserable, you liked
to pile aspersions on our lives: *full*
of trouble, devoid of pleasure. I hear you

as I used to hear my father's
*goddamnitall*s and *to hell with it*s
as he stood by the medicine cabinet

that housed his whisky bottle,
waiting there self-cursing till his drunk
could take.

    &c. _____ &c.

Life, you said, was a disagreeable thing
so you'd decided to spend it
reflecting on it.

Smear it, more likely. Turn it
against itself, like a psychometaphysical
autoimmune disorder. Autoantibodies

in the bloodstream
tearing cell from cell, as if
they had entered only to destroy.

That deepenmarrowed
muttering
these tissues which at bottom ought not to be . . .

    &c. _____ &c.

It isn't you I'm praising, you get that, don't you,
you who wanted
so fervidly

to *be* praised
for your "prize-winning essays"
when yours was the only entry,

whose publisher told you he feared
he was only printing wastepaper.
Your mother wrote, "Dear Arthur,

you are not an evil human;
you are nevertheless irritating and unbearable . . .
thus as you are, you are highly annoying."

She kept telling you your books would sit
in stacks unread,
and she was, if not maternal, at least right.

I'm reading you now, though: your "prize-winning essay"
on the Will. Highly annoying
thus as you still are.

&c. _____ &c.

The Will's your demiurge:
preexistent, unbegotten.
You say your rosaries on it:
Dolorous Mystery, Dolorous Mystery, Dolorous Mystery.

&c. _____ &c.

Life is good, you thought,
at teaching us

not to want it.

That's a lesson I keep learning
and forgetting, like a test

I'd flunk the day after I aced it.
  &c. _____ &c.

What's the matter, Schopenhauer, after
a hundred and fifty years of being dead, isn't
anything yet mattering

enough? They found a planet yesterday
without a solar system, drifting through the cosmos,
unloosed from orbit's Will.

I thought of you. Said a little prayer.
Tohu bohu, it went. *Tohu bohu*
tohu bohu, waste and void,

void and waste. I don't know who heard me. The Will's
still implacable
as any god.

Looking Down the Cliff, with Schopenhauer, on Black Friday

&c. _____ &c.

> . . . *all good things are vanity, the world in all its ends bankrupt, and life*
> *a business that does not cover its expenses.*
>
> —Schopenhauer
>
> *Post-Thanksgiving, 2012*

There's no Black Friday for you, Schopenhauer. No Good one either.
This Friday's called Black because not till then
do the box stores finally realize their first profits.
One month a year redeems their balance sheets.
Three-and-a-half seasons of hyperhyped sales
hiring firing getting spending
earn them not a penny until now.

And *that's* just retail. The rest of what we do's
just as thankless to you. *Human existence has entirely*
the character not of a gift, but of a debt.
You're welcome. We spend our lives paying at the balance,
you say, in daily increments of misery, want, but only
hold in bare abeyance the surge of interest:
the principal always stays there, massed, untouchable.

+/-

The lame duck Congress is gnawing itself again.
Here comes the Fiscal Cliff: they've got
to cut a hundred billion from the budget
and raise taxes five hundred billion, or else
we're "off the cliff," which means

budget cuts of a hundred billion,
five hundred billion in taxes.
The cuts, the taxes, both kill jobs, and joblessness
drives the deficit right back up.

The cure's the disease's etiology. It's cliff
on cliff every way we turn. Your merchant father
threw himself, when you were seventeen,
to his death from his own warehouse
into the ice-choked canal, floated there
among the slow-shoved bergs. Mine
went off a cliff when I was a teenager,
his second bankruptcy finalized the day before.

+/-

I've got an interest payment due
right now: a draft
of want, a little
collection-agency-bill of dread-thrum down the nerves.
I pay them, but they arrive and arrive again all day.

+/-

I like to read, aloud, the latest number
on the Treasury website's Debt Clock:
$16,338,092,943,716.61
and rising a trillion a year.
I could post
a Schopenhauerian debt clock
of my own to show
exactly how far in arrears our lives are,
how much suffering and anxiety outstrip
the paltry revenues of pleasure.

+/-

Let's *go* over the cliff, my reckless senator says.
Republicans won't raise taxes by a cent. They've signed a *Pledge.*
The Democrats won't cut a dollar from Medicare,
Medicaid, Social Security,
and anyway get ravaged by Republicans if they do.

Social Security, conservatives say, costs us
three-quarters of the deficit. Liberals say it doesn't cost a thing.
There's a "Trust Fund" with trillions hoarded in it
to compensate for every yearly lack
but, like God, no one can agree if it exists.

+/-

The mind has mountains, cliffs of fall,
Hopkins said. *Count them cheap*
may who ne'er hung there.
You never didn't hang there; I've got
a toe or two along the crag.
We're deep in the red, Schopenhauer, don't even know
what would count, on our balance sheets, as black.
Even the usual pleasures you mark
in gashes of red, like a teacher's
irritable correctives. However you parse it
the profit margin's slim.

The House is talking of cutting hundreds of billions
from the safety net, won't say
which billions they mean. The cliffcrags cut deep.

+/-

Black Friday. The stores, at dawn, unclang
their cages, and the blessed month of black
comes on, and on, its margins etched on every side with red.

45

THE LAST GOOD

You can reboot, in Windows, into
last known good configuration.
Whatever malicious rootkits and trojans

have misconfigured the system,
letting viruses cloak themselves and allow
a "catastrophic configuration change,"

vanish, overwritten
by the most recent state
the system can remember as Good.

I would do that to my life, wouldn't you,
harrow all the incrusting
contaminants of *waste and void* with some

stabs of uncoding like the first
downdrench of light?
I *used* to think everything was Willed,

was as it was for all good
but never-determinable cause.
Every bit of suffering and malice took its place

in some cryptic superstructure we can't see
because we're parts of it, like the Crypt
of the Resurrection in Rome

where fifty human skulls flank, as a two-columned arch,
the painting of a shock-
green-robed Christ

summoning Lazarus,
as though by his roots,
out of the earth.

We were, I thought, each like one of those skulls
holding our place in some grand
and necessary paradoxical structure, meaning

the very opposite
of the bone-matter it's made of, resurrection
in a Baroque framework of the corpse.

We couldn't know, I knew,
what we were frames for, or where the emptied hourglasses were flying
on their wings built from human shoulderbones.

Now I think we're more like another skeleton:
of the carrier pigeon from D-Day found
among rubbish and twigs in a Surrey chimney

decades later, its message to Allied headquarters
tied still in a scarlet capsule on its legbone.
No one now remembers

what it meant.
We won't ever decrypt ourselves,
Schopenhauer: to us it's just

HVPKD, KLDTS,
strapped on a little remnant
of soot-stuck clawbone.

"I Don't Like My Soul Parts"

&c. _____ &c.

You see there's an Arthur Schopenhauer,
often, in my mind,
muttering his strings

of cosmoscidal et ceteras.
I write this twist
of psalm to still

him instead of you,
you who are gone
into that unbeing

you so voluminously and erotically extolled.

READING *THE PURPOSE DRIVEN LIFE*, WITH SCHOPENHAUER

&c. _____ &c.

—Rick Warren, *The Purpose Driven Life: What On Earth Am I Here For?*

Really—I don't know what the meaning or purpose of life is.
But it looks exactly as if something were meant by it.
—Carl Jung

December 2012

I.

The Truth will make us miserable, Rick Warren says. That sounds like you,
Schopenhauer. It's OK, though, because all our miseries
are *Father-filtered*: The Lord wills them, slips them through.
God will bake our afflictions like a cake, take
the bitter taste of oil and eggyolks and raw flour
and stir them into harmony, just so.
We tried to bake my mother a birthday cake
when I was a kid. I don't know what went wrong
but that batter rose in a lopsided tumor
over the pan's sides then burst open, with a fetid
cloud so acrid we buried the whole mess in the backyard.

I'm not saying the Lord will make of *our*
sufferings that kind of botched concoction, but still:
there are cakes and there are cakes.
And miseries, however Father-filtered, purpose-shrivel.
This morning I reused the coffee filter, pouring new
grounds over the old; the used ones clumped the bottom and clogged the way
and the water just massed there, in the paper, a blacksludged stew.

Rick Warren says life is a test, and once we know that
we will never feel insignificant again.
But my life-test Study Guide feels
like it's on a grayed-out link. I click it anyway.
I copy and paste the URL into three different browsers;
they try so hard to sound human, saying *Oops!* and *Oh snap!*
So I have to write the questions for myself, like
in one of those experimental high schools.

Rick Warren's chapters are structured on 40 days and 40 nights
to learn The Five Purposes of Our Lives.
I write each Purpose out on a 3 x 5 notecard.
They get confused, though: is
to be a magnifier of his glory the same
as *to give him pleasure?*
They're both listed as Purpose Three.
The first is to give God pleasure (wait,
this can't be right); the third to become like Christ.
You missed those both, Schopenhauer.
I can't even read my scribble-card on the second one.

You liked the burial beetle as an instance
of nature's profligate
futility. So: Pleasure is to life as burial beetles are
to what? The carcass
into which they lay their eggs, whose flesh
they scoop and eat and feed their larvae?
If the world were a paradise of luxury and ease
men would (a) feel replete with Purpose and thanksgiving
or—you should know this one, Schopenhauer,
you wrote it—: (b) either
die of boredom or hang themselves.

III

We must offer up the *sacrifice of thanksgiving*, says the Psalm. Listen
with me for its fat-hiss and flare; sniff
the sizzled clawlike curl
of its charred meat.
To *give* thanks you have to have
them first. *Get* them. Wherever you can. Pleasure
must be taken. We will take it. We will take it again and again.

Take notes with me, Schopenhauer, for lo
these 40 nights and 40 days.
This book sold 32 million in hardback.
We'll find our purpose there, together. Especially now.
There's been another massacre; twenty first graders
mowed down in ten minutes in their classroom.
The President says we must *take meaningful action*
but hasn't said yet what meaningful might mean.

I've been taking, Schopenhauer, unmeaningful actions,
going back and forth to Rite Aid
for wrapping paper, Christmas cards, mailing boxes, little migraine-strobing crèches.
I keep forgetting what I came for. Keep forgetting
the difference between a ritual and a compulsion and a rite.
I keep wondering if *Mass* and *massacre* have some common root.
All the way there and back the radio
alternates Snoop Dogg Christmas carols
(*On the second day of Christmas my homeboy gave to me*
a fifth of hendog to take my mind off that weed)
with news flashes of the children
led with eyes closed past the piles of bullet-riddled bodies.
I'm OK, Mommy, but all my friends are dead.
By the time I got to the drugstore I was thinking
of the defunct rite of Extreme Unction, of what good
any unction could be in this extremis:

I saw the Rite Aid sign and for an instant wondered
if it was us in need of aid from those lost rites
or the rites themselves that needed help.

V.

A small parenthesis in eternity—Rick Warren's quoting Sir Thomas Browne—
our lives are a small parenthesis in eternity.
They stand in apposition, interjective; we're like
a little piece of a Faulkner sentence, a crowded (oblivious and much-stuffed)
aside. What's kept inside there doesn't even know
the rest of the syntax
it interrupts. It
thinks it's the whole sentence, the whole
luststrewn, Time-mournful, Faulknerian sprawl.

VI.

Don't be troubled by trouble, Rick Warren says. He's pithy that way.
We need hope to cope. God uses our problems to draw us
closer to Himself. We're near now, my Lord, *this* Christmas, we're near.
God uses sledgehammers on us, jackhammers, wrecking balls,
whatever it takes to reach us.
Apparently, Bushmaster AR-15 semiautomatic rifles, with 30-round magazines, too.
We must become *better, not bitter. God never wastes a hurt.*

Everybody's looking for some purpose
behind Adam Lanza's rampage.
He couldn't make Eye Contact. He didn't bathe. He played Call of Duty hour
    after hour.
He was jealousy-enraged against his mother's students, except
she wasn't ever a teacher. The purposes behind the massacre
make no sense; still it looks
exactly as if something were meant by it.

This December the hurts are everywhere, laid waste. Stir,
Lord, like Ezekiel, their
clumsily reassembling dry bones.

VII.

We're all in Warm-Ups, Schopenhauer, in spring training. Pick a metaphor
for preamble. Larvae with regurgitated
shrew-corpse-flesh in their mouths. Life's not the thing
but its precursor. We're resident
aliens, Warren says, with "spiritual green cards."
We're temp workers, like the ones
laid off each year by Walmart so they don't qualify for pensions.

So this is the mudroom, with its
bootsmudges and strew of sopped wool.
These years are the undergarments, their Infinity-enwrapped flash and frill.
This life is the foreplay, tongueflit on the clit.

The point is, we can't get the point.
We're unhomed here, unhomely.
Our pleasure's never the point.
It's God whose pleasure counts. We're here
to please Him. That's our First Purpose. He watches us
while we sleep. He sniffs and licks His lips.
The point is this is Forever-Practice. The point's
invisible, interred. We'll unbury it in Eternity —come
with me, Schopenhauer, drive the point
in, let it
pierce and pierce us, now,

then then.

PART III
HYMENEAL

Nuptial Song

I.

The lyrebird's on his tumulus again, scratching
out his song
made all of mimic-music, the strung-

together mating chirrs
of butcherbird and honeyeater.
Midwinter,

their mating's long
over so they're muted now
(fled is that music)

and the winterbreeder
lyrebird makes the snatches of his song
out of their diminished things,

their beak-snaps and feather-beats,
kookaburra's chortle, scraps
of echolalic trill: lifts

the sinuous
lyre-bow shape of his plumage
and buries his drab

turkeylike body beneath
the silver shock of its underfeathers
and lets burst loose from that shimmer his spoils:

whipbird whipcrack catbird screech, the cockatoo's green
freedoms of improvisational
innuendo. Winter

is icumen in. Cuccu
nu. Sing cuccu. Nu cuccu. Jug
jug. Tereu. Lhude

sing. Lewd-sing. Al-
lude-and-loud sing. A *lied*'s
what's sung. An air's a song, and what the song moves

through, polyglot
and monomaniacal. Make me thy lyre. Bare ruin'd choirs
where late the lyrebirds lied.

II.

Listen, the song's all over. Split
the lyrebird and you'll find
no music (silverrolled) only

filaments of feather, and a lyre-
interred, self-secreting face.
Lyrebird, what thou art

we know not, so many
other melodies involved
in what we know: mellifluous

cacophonies
of simulacrum. Teach us
what scherzos

and staccatos might be
pilfered and still
all thine (be thou

me, bethou me): hail
to thee, blithe duper, to
thy lyre-bedraggled plumes.

III.

He drags them through the dirt,
dug-
up grub-litter

on the mating mound he's scratched
open like a tomb
while the lyre-hen

witnesses tail-shimmer
and vine-yank till the forest shakes,
and the "lyrebird-specific whistle" intermerges

with rapidrip of mimicry
(The tangled bine-stems scored the sky / Like strings of broken lyres) . . .
One hypothesis says he shrieks

the most strenuous songs he's heard to show
his mastery of syrinx
muscles' hard striations,

but what she wants with such
vocal virtuosity
no theorist can tell. Mimicry

itself may be, one says,
of no evolutionary
relevance after all. Darkling,

still, she listens. The achieve
of, the mastery of the thing.
The bird would *be as*

other birds. Singing
not to sing. His melody
absorbs into itself each frequency:

camera shutter car alarm
dingo-bark and chainsaw-shrill
so all his mind's mimesis and the mimed

falls irrecoverable into
all-encompassing hymeneal song.
I was single

and pervious in my mind
like a mound
on which there was one lyrebird

who mimicked of winter, in full-
throated ease, trilling
the inflections

of a locomotive's
chuff and steam whistle, a baby's
caterwaul, and the long declension of all my silence afterwards.

ON MARRIAGE

I.

Wind's the medium of air.
It says what in the air's
stasis we'd never hear.
In the sibilation of its leaving
it says what air would say
(the kinesis of that silence)
if stationary atmosphere
could scrape, stridulous,
itself against its unmoving self.

II.

Wind's air
that sensed a near
hollow in the pressure

and poured
toward that rising stratum
to hold it fast: a depression

in the balance
of things it had to change

itself to fill.

III.

Still air's
wind that had its way, inrushed, unemptied
what was left, then settled

into the lull it was, its
constituent quiescence:

immotive, as if straining
not to quiver toward each new
instability of heat along the edges—
the still of its want; the want
motivating all its still.

ANTITHALAMION

Now will come the bride, now will the Hymen-song be sung
—Catullus

I.

As Hymen is
to nuptial bed: the god of it, and

what must be gotten rid of
for their pleasure.

II.

They were under a certain flower: say, lobelia—

the garden book spoke of its
"terminal clusters"—

They were under a certain
planet's influence: Saturn's, say;

the depression-book called it
beglooming, taciturn,

ice-ringed . . .

III.

Would no one
listen at least till the couplet's

rhyme-end
that would have made it what

it was to be

Skin-fringe, perforate, semilunar,

the hymen has,
say Masters and Johnson, *no evident function*—

V.

To her he was as far now
as apostate
from apostle,

as *vertex* from *vortex*

VI.

To love
the word
sunder, but not
the sundering it means

and the *harrowing*
of Hell, but only if
to harrow means

in that case to plough

VII.

Omega's
seeds everywhere blown
over alpha's plowrows

VIII.

There they were, at altar, all vow and vowel: *do.*
Here they are, all altered, dis-
sonant and undervotive: *done.*

Say them some requiescat,
say to them: Do you take this
antonym's antonym, this homologous de-
voting:
do us

part.

IX.

Caesura's a cut
          a halving

A *sense pause*   down the middle
where the   gist went.

X.

The paired gray   and reddish bodies
the "dual-lobed   mass" of the thalamus
lie close   astride the cleft
at the brain's   innermost chamber
consummation-place   where sense gets made
of the senses,   what the nerves bring on—

vaginal-spread in sagittal section
lobed and lipped: the thalamus

named by Galen for the bed-
chamber outside which the bridal party

65

would gather to intone their wedding song

that her cries might not be heard   when the hymen breaks.

What Do You Think the Poet Is Trying to Say?

My son's denaturing. I'm trying to say
he's experimenting with irreversible reactions.
Fifteen, stressed over his Biology, he's letting hydrochloric acid
do its work on eggwhites, break the weak
linkages in their native conformations.
It's a simple thing, he's learning, to disrupt
the original bonds that hold the proteins in place;
a little whipping can make the alpha helixes
permanently unfurl. The result's discoloration and a clump
of sudden coagulants. The looser go the bonds the more
grotesque the shapes denaturing leaves behind.
I show him milk I warmed at 3 a.m.
for my insomnia, the strings of mucid curdles
it formed the minute I turned the gasflame on.
That's denaturing too. The insomnia-milk
smelled fine; who could tell it had gone so bad
till the slightest heat made it skin
over in its spoil. I'm trying, in what ways I know, to say
nature's got its own means of forming looser bonds.
I like the kinds of bonds odd words can make.
Inspissate's just the one for what was in that pan,
word viscid and opaque as the thickening it means.
My son's denaturing. I'm straining to say
he's loose these days with acid to our tertiary bonds.
He likes, when he drops the corrosive in,
the clabber and discolor of albumen
that's only there to protect the yolk.
He's *inchoate* at fifteen, meaning
"imperfectly formed; commenced
but not completed; partially done." The denatured
proteins rearrange themselves in random
and unpredictable new shapes and bonds, says his Study Guide.
I've been trying very hard to say I love
the word *inchoate*, and the inchoation of words, the way

sometimes they feel sticky with their birth-slime.
I love them when they're incipient, inspissate:
inchoate's got the Latin for "hitch up"
deep in its protein structure. It started out to mean
"The strap fastened to the oxen's yoke": to begin
is to hitch the plow. I love—I'm trying to say—to say
"strap fastened to the oxen's yolk," don't you.
Aah aah, ah oh. Inchoate song. Turn
the plow. I keep trying to say I like the way
yoke and *yolk* clump together when you say them.
Like how *like* clumps too. I like
how the eggwhite slithers away and leaves
the yolk's inchoate glisten and quiver in the hand.
Inchoate's got *inch* in its look and *ink*
in its sound, like the inching-forth
of the ink, its inchoation, its heavy dragging
turn and re-turn of the plow. It's a thick and difficult
thing, this trying-to-say to someone you love. It's gutterals
and glottal stops and fricatives and friction. It's leaving
the unsaid in there, too, part always of what pulls the plow.
Note your observations—the Study Guide asks—as the bonds begin
to disintegrate. The milk scums over. The son
shouts and throws across the room
his book of oblique and indetermined angles
in little rows marked *x* and *y*. The yolk
is safe from its denatured white. The yoke groans. *Words*
I know what to do with. My son's
denaturing, by which I've been trying to say
he's strapping oxen to the plowyoke, setting off and off to start.
How is opacity often—the Study Guide asks—the first
sign of a denaturing? How do you think a poem
denatures words, lets their alpha helixes uncoil,
vowels sour and clump, their inspissate meanings
run through every fissure in our fists?
What do *you* think the poet is trying
and trying and trying and trying not to say
when he calls his son from geometry-fume into the kitchen
and splatters into a pan already smoking on the stove

the not-obviously-turned but much-too-quick-
to-curdle-and-denature squirt of milk,
leaving its grainy furrows through the spoil?

The Name of the Island Was Marriage

for Suzanne

I.

The name of the island was Island and the name of the Friday
was Good. Sunflower roots lay smoked on a bed of moss

over sea-flattened stones and sealed in a cedar box, like a tiny
coffin on the china: the unpent

smoke outpuffed its alderwood burn on our cheeks.
The constituents of a thirty-year marriage

lay before us, like a mis-en-place:
ingredients of pleasure, local

and strange. We assembled them as if we had never
used them before, like the raw

deer hearts strewn with wildflowers, pearls
of herring roe scooped up on branches of hemlock.

Stinging nettles, sweet, long-roasted: where,
where now was their sting?

II.

To name an island for the very idea
of an island: its insularity, its

nonnegotiable unfluidity.
All pent in by what it is not—

the restless aqueous—so its name
insisted it was what it was.

The name of the marriage had come to be Angry Teen.
The name of the marriage had come to be Did We Fuck Up.

Skunk cabbage burst all over from the roadside murk,
more xanthic than sunflowers or than noon sun, more

skunk-scent-insistent than skunks. *The decedents
of the earliest settlers,* said the typo, *still live on the island today.*

So the dead walk here, all
pent in by what they are not.

III.

The island was Island Island. The god
was I AM WHO I AM. As

in the beginning He made each thing, it seemed
to startle Him to realize

it was good, as if *good*
were something else He gave birth by merely

having it in His mind.
Glimmers of saltwater poured off clay and marl

and *dry* was born. Island lay isolate, not-wet
in the wet. *Is land* was born.

We smoothed the marred
crust of what we'd made, and

the idea of *marriage* was reborn, the idea
of *marring* unborn.

IV.

The chef came to our room to fix the unstoppable furnace.
He smelled of sorrel and roasted oysters and sage as he knelt

to fiddle with the gas-blast. *Dolce far niente* painted on the wall. The sweet
achievement of nothing.

Only when God began to *do,* after untimeable stasis,
did He find out how good

His pouring-apart of opposites—sunrip and earth, up-
tick of skunk cabbage and its stench, and

sunflower root and the box of dark it huddled in—might be.
Let us divide *decedents*

from *descendent,* motherfather from son. Somewhere, even here, a furious
angel struggles in air to aim his chalice

exactly to catch each blood-spurt off the cross.
It must be saved. In three days the decedent will live

again and want back His blood. The island's name
in some no-longer translatable tongue was said

to *be* Island, as if island
were all that an island could be. The name of the marriage, as if

we *made* it, by calling it, so
was said—behold, it startles us still—to be good.

Bruce Beasley, *Offspring*

OFFSPRING INSPRUNG

for my son Jin
after Bruce Beasley's sculpture Offspring

I like to take shapes that . . . by their intersecting of each other start to talk to us emotionally . . .
I want you to see these penetrations, because there are wonderful secondary shapes that happen.
—Bruce Beasley the sculptor

I. _____
Look with me, Jin, at *Offspring*. Each cube-half-insunk-in-cube
is unsuccessive, broken-off, or -in. Violable. Each outbursts
from its parent but leaves part of itself—a quarter-face, a vertex—
unseeably behind there. Its cubeship only emerges deep within
what fathers it, insprung in the cube it topples and lurches to emerge
out of—and that shape (sideswiped, foundering) will never let it go.

II. _____
Here the crystalline invanishings, the way a part of the self might interrupt
and incomplete the rest, intelling itself to itself, ambiguating unrevealable
faces. Here these heaped, thick-patina'd cubes (a man who has my name
sent them to me) in lopsided ascension, their innerlap and off-tilt and up-
tumble. His heaped bronzes involute themselves into my words, intercut
my offspring son insprung now into cryptoshapes of adolescence, their outjuts.

III. _____
Each cube would be *of* another cube, or two, or four, so inters
itself within them, genitive. In*ter*, from *terra*, earth, earth interred
in the very word. Let these terraruptions stand for you, Jin, and me,
inmixed: each burial makes the cube's form dissipate, unknowable
unless we imagine it as some conceivable but inexistent innerness,
occultation of inviolable underform deep in the subbronze.

IV. _____
Your parents are parenthetical to you now, Jin, in
temporary apposition—what closes us off barely

74

interrupts your syntax. I was fifteen, like you, when
a stroke took my father; for two years I'd been subformed
so deep in myself he used to beg me to say *anything*
to him, ask me over and over if I'd gone mute.

V. _____

"But the part of a cube that penetrates
out of another cube is no longer a cube,"
says the man of bronze who has my name.
Overtly clandestine no-longer-cube, Jin, where's *your* face, I've barely
seen it in a week, you're omissive, uptumbling like these forms, im-
partible, indiscerptible: who can see into the penetralia, who you are.

VI. _____

As though a pile of dice had come to rest, die-interpenetrating-
die so we can't even read the dots their cleromance reveals.
Their message recondite as the past and undivulgable
as the geometry of What's-to-Come, the past's uncontrollable
offspring—six facets of the future interrupted and secretly
fulfilled as dice that spring from out and tumble deep within it.

VII. _____

Homoousian comes crawling from the dictionary: doctrine
that the Father and the Son are of one substance, One-in-Being.
I like to turn *Offspring* upside down, on my desk, see it lurch, watch
how gravity rejects the foundation block not stabilizing its offspring.
Abstract; there's just dissemblance there: unlikeness. We're homoousian,
Jin, we're One in Being. So close as to be, sometimes, *closed.*

VIII. _____

I've got my father in me, his offspringing shape
closed in there, so implicated in the cubes that make me
not one of his faces or mine is uninterrupted, and two lie
almost completely merged inside. The prayer goes *Intra*

tua vulnera absconde me. Father: are you in me, are you mute,
hide me in your woundedness, hide me in your vulnera.

IX. _____

This is my Fraction Rite, the riving of these cubes. Like the moment in Mass
when you hear a crack as the lifted Host is split in two, meaning the broken
body of the god. Into His vulnera. Meaning bread-turned-flesh, flesh-into-cut
Lord. I've been thinking of adoring the Eucharist. They need adorers at 3 a.m.,
says the Bulletin. To venerate continuously what suffers itself into what it
isn't. "I want you to see these penetrations," my doppleganger says. Me too. Me too.

X. _____

It figures, Bruce, I'd do this—turn your shapes,
pyritic and self-permeable, into words, with
all language's pregnable figurings of speech.
It figures I'd make their outsurgings stand
for more literal springings-loose: myself from
my father, Jin from me, me from unwordable you.

XI. _____

Go ahead, Jin: Murmur curses as you kick the door.
Stab one jagged vertex out of the fathering cube.
Three faces collide there: your mother's; mine; where's yours,
oh that one, the little spike, the one that's just outbarbed,
the one that feels inhumed by the very shapes that bronze-
swaddled it in the first place, to keep it safe. *Fucking assholes.*

XII. _____

These interpenetrations like infixes, what stabs itself into the middle
of a word to alter everything it means. Like your birth parents, Jin:
always secretly intervolving, covert fulfillment of the cube's missing
vertices and edges. Cube root: two other multiples of yourself, two
withinward faces, who are you, and are muted, those intimate planes
contiguous with yours, delineaments of which you haven't yet known.

XIII and XIV.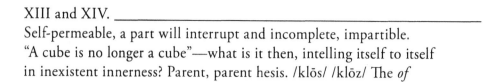
Self-permeable, a part will interrupt and incomplete, impartible.
"A cube is no longer a cube"—what is it then, intelling itself to itself
in inexistent innerness? Parent, parent hesis. /klōs/ /klōz/ The *of*

> It figures, words, I'd do this, hide myself
> inside your vulnera, turn your shapes
> upside down and inside out, in lopsided
> ascension, lurching to emerge. Go ahead,
> words, call me. Who *are* you? Who *has* my name? Me,
> ambiguated. Earth interred in *earth*, and terrarupting.

of a genitive, a generation. The *sever* locked in. Absconde me. Invanquish,
-vanish. One-in-Being, come crawling out. Unconceal these forms. Gravity
rejects the very foundation. This foundering. The mind can't help. Spring loose.

XV. _____
So not the spheres' music but the cubes' cacophonies—
Sometimes words get haptic, available to touch. *Cacophonies. Haptic.*
Infix. Occultate. That's their outerrupting: the *sever* locked in *several*,
and fighting its way back out. If words could unconceal their forms,
severable, like the *of* of a genitive: the love *of* a father. Inalienably possessing, meaning
the fathering and sonship can never—no matter how concealed the faces get—be
    severed.

PART IV
THE SIXTH DUST

Revised Catechism

ON PRAYER

Say what is a prayer.
Outhiss and foam-spurt from a spent
hairspray can, trash-spilled,

when you puncture its side with a pitchfork
just to hear what it might say.

Under what conditions must we formulate our prayers?
As though a leper's scabbed lips
unswelled enough for speech.

How shall we have confidence our prayers have been heard?
Kneeler-scrape
across the oakgrain floor:

gash the supplicant's weight
scars between the pews.

ON CATECHISM

Where shall our satisfaction reside: in the restlessness of our questions, or in their satiation?
As the orb-weaver hangs—concentered in the whorls of its finished spiral web—
between raspberry canes, its spinnerets empty.

Say whether the answers themselves might still be errable.
Hollow in the raspberry, scarlet-juice-brimmed, where the stem has just fallen away.

Might we build a foundation on what, nevertheless, shadows-forth to confound us?
As the orb-weaver hangs—concentered in the whorls of its finished spiral web—
between raspberry canes, its spinnerets empty.

ON PRAYER

How might our prayers be expected to alter the will of God?
As surf-foam clings
to stringers of kelp
yanked seaward, then shoreward,

that settle in a receding
streamlet the moment the tide
no longer can reach them.

ON CATECHISM

May we question also that which is not dubitable?
Should the spider's legs stick to its own capture silk?
Does the spider consume, each night, the orb of its web, to furnish
again the very silk it will need to rebuild it?

Cleft for Me Let Me Hide Myself from Thee

Qui diceris Paraclitus
(O Comforter, to Thee we cry)
—"Veni, Creator Spiritus"

Come, Comforter.
I strain
toward your inrushing arrow as it halves

then halves then halves
the distance that severs us.
Till Kingdom

comes its Zeno-arrow lurches
in time lapse, not
still where it was, nor yet in that place where it is not.

†| |†

Come to me, Paraclitus, across
trillions of synaptic clefts, leave
where they lie

the molecules of my consoling:
norepinephrine, dopamine, cast
as charred

offerings into the voltaic
gap between us. Synapse: apse. Semi-domed
recessive altars, almost touching. Come, Untouchable, from the other side.

†| |†

Come at me, Comforter, but noli
me tangere, stay
on the dendrite's side of that infinit-

esimal fissure between
herenow and Kingdom Come, like the cleft
where Moses cowered

in the rock while the cleaving
obliterating Lord-glory
passed him by . . .

†| |†

Come, Uncomforter.
Some prayer ferries over the cerebrospinal fluid
(nearer-my-god, nearer) zeroing
in

on Your ever-called-for unarrival.

†| |†

There's a hole in us, says Pascal, shaped like God.
It can only be refilled by what's infinite, what's
hole-shaped itself and long-torn-away.

I run my fingers over and over
my temples, feeling
under skull-ridges for the brain

riddled with the rifts
cleft there as Thee.

Such and Such and Such and Such

When emptiness works then everything in existence works;
if emptiness does not work, then all existence does not work.

—Nagarjuna

I.

I can't stop watching the YouTube of these moon jellies
yanking their translucence inside out
over and over and getting
nowhere—with their four

scarlet gonads shockingly opaque,
seen-right-through-to, like a neon cross
throbbing inside the palpable
transparence of their unsubstance . . .

They tighten and loosen into structures
of blob
that pulse them ever closer to the surface,
all mouthparts and hanging tentacles

studded with stingers.
And breathe by drawing oxygen
right through their bodies' flimsy borders.
Their phylum name means "hollow guts."

The water you see right through them
is ninety-five percent of all they are, so what we don't see
in seeing them *is* them, aqueous Suchness. We say
such and such to mean something particular

we don't want to say. Lobed
mucus-covered mouthlips at the underbell.
Form is emptiness, emptiness is form, says the Sutra.
Their mouth is their anus, their anus their mouth.

I reload and reload the page to remind me there are such
gut-empty things, bells
that unring themselves. Nothing, such
as they are, *but* Suchness: sacs of lack.

II.

It is said that the world is empty, the world is empty, Lord.
In what respect is it said to be empty?
All these new words for the *suchness* of the empty:
sunyata, tathata, anatma—mindfill of them.

When the world is viewed as sunya, empty,
it is grasped in its Suchness. What Suchness
the molddust and tristitched binding and semiopaque
overleafs of *Seventy Verses on Emptiness*

have rubbed against my thumbs.
Tathata is the absoluteness of sunya. How's that?
The polyp strobilates to produce ephyra. Come again?
And there they come again, filling the full screen

in my mind with such mucilaginous
blue and throbbing phosphorescent slime.
Of how empty even Emptiness is, the thinkers
mull. If meanings, they say, were "nondifferent"

from their signs, the word *fire* would burn our mouths,
rip its singe through the page.
No Self here, just the usual five senses and the Mind—
the "Six Dusts." I breathe them in. Especially the Mind,

that allergen. The jellies only glow when they're annoyed,
their irritance their luminance. They have no mind.
A "subumbrellar nerve net" makes their coronal
muscle tighten and release, release and tighten

like the heart they haven't.
They're never not in motion, but only go
where the current takes them. All their ex-umbrellar
self-inversions only keep them, glowing, near the surface.

Yet there's such relentless
haecceitas about their
gelatinous, self-everting
mesoglea with its pink

gonads and frills. *Haecceitas*: that's *Thisness*. Is that
nondifferent from Suchness?
Who makes a doctrine of Emptiness, says the Buddha,
is incurable. Of what am I incurable, Lord?

With knowledge of things in their state of Suchness
the mind becomes pure and free
of the fissures of division . . .
This morning I didn't split, with my thumbnail, the Effexor

tablet in half—I ate it whole. Now such Emptiness
inverts itself. There's a place in the brain
called ventromedial cortex where significance gets made—
turn it down and the Six Dusts

go dull and empty, turn it up and everything's replete
with meaning, hypergraphia, as if the word
fire were to blaze on the lips like a coal, the letters of *suchness*
contract their coronal muscles and outend

their subumbrella, stingered blob.
Little Squalicum Beach below me now is nothing
but fissures of division: breakwaters
in wind-rips outturning their translucence,

foaming into Suchness on the stones
self-crushed against themselves,
splitting the spume into aquagreen
over such a lightning-interruptive sunstruck gold.

IV.

That suffering = life, and life
suffering, I get. Impermanence,
that's easy. The Sixth Dust, the brain's own fissures, slivers
the world into all its smashed-up thoughts.

Emptiness: I think I've got
a tight grip
on that one.
Would I have me be

like these
jellies, emptying myself
of myself,
spewing that waste through my mouth?

I'm curable, Lord.
This morning I looked down the railroad bridge
and didn't wonder how far the average suicide
must jump to do the job. That Suchness.

"I am currently in despair" should not be asserted.
"I am not currently in despair" should not be asserted.
"I am currently both in and not in despair" should not be asserted.
"I am currently neither in nor not in despair" should not be asserted.

"Suffering and Suchness are nondifferent"
should neither be written, nor not-written.
"The soul is as divisible as a worm
and crawls from itself, as itself" should neither be said

nor not-said. There is no nonempty "I" here to say.
Moon jellies *are* the water
through which and out of which and into
which they throb and throb and come again toward the surface and breathe.

PART V
THE MASS OF THE ORDINARY

Ordinary: the order of divine service, esp. that of the Mass; the established order or form for saying mass; the service of the Mass
—Oxford English Dictionary

Kyrie

Out of the ordinary summer keeps insisting
on its antirarefaction,
its teem and refusal to be culled.

Out of the ordinary the buried things keep
coming back, inordinate, like the white
nerve-net of raspberry roots I almost yanked
out of rainblown earth on my roof,
the gutters bursting with their spiked canes.

Come now, World-to-Come, are You really there.
Now-here there's word-spilth, weed-creep
down the eaves, common

and improper as nouns.
Suzanne called up from the lawn, *Well, do they
have any berries?*—wanting,
like Christ at the fig tree,
to leave them rooted
deep between the shingles, if only they bore.

World-to-Come, You're late. You're other-
wise, You're elsewhere, like the word
verb, meaning
just the part of speech it isn't.

Today I flunked the Oxford Happiness Test.
I could not strongly agree
that *I feel able to take*
anything on.
Or disagree
that *I am not especially in control.*
There was *a gap between what I would like*
to do and what I have done.
I didn't *feel particularly pleased*
with the way I am.

Lord have mercy Christ have mercy Lamb of God have
mercy—

Kyrie
eleison, Lord: are You
particularly pleased with the way I am?

———————————————

Have mercy, Lord, the way
a dog will have its fleas, inrunning
through tracks of gnawed fur, as outward
and visible sign
of inner summer. Paw-smack and whimper. Have

mercy, Lord, the way these downspouts
overhang with what lays down roots
in their improbable dirt,
teeming, refusing to self-
cull, and means,
in spite of every propriety,

to stay.

EMBOLISM

. . . protect us from all anxiety as we wait in joyful hope for the coming of our Savior . . .

They used to say *why* in the middle

of a sentence, caesural,
interruptive with wonder, like:
When I was a young man, why, I felt pretty happy.

The Why took its place at the crux. Like the zero
that always severs
the positive and negative integers,

like Moses at the Red Sea,
astride what he sunders.

Right smack in the middle, my student said
of the genitalia on Roman nudes:
You're trying to enjoy a masterpiece, and there it always is,
right smack in the middle, completely spoiling the view.

Galen thought the brain released a swarm called *pneuma,*
a soul-stuff out of the eyes
that made the atmosphere around us perceptive,
electric, ennerving and enbraining all the air
till the pneuma reflock and fly back through the crystalline lens
to give the brain tidings of what's out there.

Light from
light's repulsion off a mass:
It's the *in*visible things that interest me right now,

Maker, among
summer's compulsive bodiments.

———————————

What's that you're mumbling, Epictetus,
deep in the back of my brain,
swaddled in swarms of pneuma,
completely spoiling the view?:
*Never say about anything, 'I have lost it'; say
'I have given it back.'
Is your child dead? It has been given back.
Is your wife dead? She has been given back.*

———————————

What wavelength, Light-from-Light, are You on?

Anything wholly lucid
light just leaves
behind.

Everything this morning seems
unseemly, unakin
to the merely ordinary smear-
mass of the way things
usually seem, and *are*.

———————————

Summer's chthonian, the
under-
neath re-
upbrought, bamboo stalks'
upstab through each fence
slat and concrete slab.

To determine your happiness level,
strongly or mildly
agree or disagree:
1. I find most things amusing.
2. I do not think that the world is a good place.

Amuse me, Things:
you seem ordinary, *of no particular interest,* now,
like a verb that means
the obverse of all doing, self-
betrayer: *Stymie. Stall.*

———————————

Melancholia's chthonian, under-
rip of amygdala's
backwash of neurotransmitted
doom-come, enbrained and restless
for exit
from this Is.
And here I'm

the apostrophe
in a contraction, little sign
of something taken out,
re-upbrought, vertically
wedged. I would give myself
back. Look for me
in the elision, what's
pulled to pieces and
left there, to self-
eradicate, regenerate
and slowly so slowly
begin to begin
to redescend.

SANCTUS

Some weeks I wake up feeling, Lord, like
the bird-dropping spider, camouflaged
as runnels of fresh birdshit on a leaf, spangle-
glisten and black-and-chalk

dimples down the vein. All the birds
think it's their own crap and won't come near.
But butterflies, "wont to settle

on the evacuations," light
right into the smear-white of its web, just
where and as it wants them to be.

I see through You, Lord,
as if You were not there.
I see through *You*, as You must see
me, like shit

that isn't what it seems.
I'm wont to settle on these evacuations,
to make a praise song of how the light
deceives us,

what shit we find
ourselves
not to be. We sing

Sanctus where we can. Maker
of all things
seen, unseen

visibilium omnium et invisibilium,
let me believe that things aren't like
their semblances.
Order ≠ ordure,

though the bird-dropping spider resembles,
in every way the human eye can evaluate,
both order and ordure from on high.

CREDO

That which is indubious
has already been negotiated.
The Period for Comments is now closed.

—I am Party to the Memorandum
of Understanding of All Things, its
codicils and paragraphs of Agreement to Agree,
yet much in it remains to me obscure.

You must first accept the Conditions and the Terms.

—I clicked the little box marked I AGREE,
unable otherwise to get
onto any further screen;
conceding, with many hesitations, to the Conditions;
at odds, though, with the very notion
of prearranged and arbitrary
limitations to the Term.

The term Term *refers, linguistically,*
to any mass of words
considered as the members of an utterance.
See the Glossary that prefaces the Preamble.

—"Members of an Utterance"? Is that what we are

when we merge with an unenumerated We
to chant, in slightly out-of-synch
and interrupting unison

"By the power of the Holy Spirit was incarnate" or
"And His kingdom shall have no end," or—

Minus grievous errors
or omissions, adjustments
to the Understanding
shall be determined by the following formula,
and only during the next Arbitration:

$$A_i = \frac{Max\left[T_{j[i],k[i]} \times 1.06^* \times (1 + Min[g(Y_i), 16] \times 0.0025) - S_i, 0\right]}{\sum_{i=1}^{N} Max\left[T_{j[i],k[i]} \times 1.06^* \times (1 + Min[g(Y_i),16] \times 0.0025) - S_i, 0\right]} \times a \times TS$$

See Appendix A for definitions of the variables.

We accede

that the Maker of all Things
Visible and Invisible

is Itself opaque-
till-shone-through, so
temporarily unbeholdable: yet We
wait in joyful hope. We—
I—believe

in It as one born
blind might in the ice
crystals in a cirrus cloud, or
in the indigo strip of a rainbow
scrimming through a low-hung fog,

his optic nerve firing nothing
down its myelin sheath, like
mist scrimming that rainbow's
fogbow-white and almost-
vanished-already violet slice.

FRACTION RITE

Solstice-swollen insomnia: its
nonordinary tempo, when I lie,
eyes open, saying Latin Mass to the cadence
of my own pulse
and day-dreads hour after hour, from
ten-thirty dusk till
four o'clock dawn:
God from God, Light from Light,
Truegod from Truegod

Deum de Deo—with every jerking systole—
Deum—with every diastole—*de Deo*
on every breath-intake.
Deum verum
de Deo vero.
With Him   all things   are made.

Blood-throb
in the temple, blood-throb in the throat.
Pneuma-swarm and -throb, seeking through the dark
something to bring back news of to the brain.

By-Whom-All-Things-Are-Made, make me again.

Then it's time
to reenter Time:
as if it were
all there were

I go before the day, its halt
processional,
the twenty-fourth

of June, the ordinal, the
relentless *th* of it.

By enlarge, my student wrote, meaning
I guess *by and large.*

By Enlarge the raspberry has lifted itself
roofward, *osanna*
in excelsis. Things blow this way, ordained
by destiny, or deity, or
Enlarge. They're *meant,* it seems, *to be,*
though no one can agree
what it is that means them.

The tidings keep arriving, not
all of them glad.
My sister has a camera
small as a pill in her gut
moving through her seeking
something bleeding.

I can't remember this time-processional even pausing

before it came to be
known instead as a *recessional,*
the colors of its banners gradually darkening
to mauve, then mauve-black like a bruise.

You are connected, my laptop tells me, *to the server Kronos.*

I have loved the strangest
words for what recurs, what's
clogged—like the gutters in raspberry brambles—with Time:
hebdomadal,
catamenial.

A *quotidian fever*: one that lasts just a day.

The chronic, the served-by-Kronos:
tedium of sequiturs, their unsurprise.

Beyond this point, said the airport sign, *you must
continue to exit.*

Kronos, jealous
all-devourer. Who swallowed
each of his infants, sent
them back into Time.

What is is what occurs, except
what's not, which also
takes its preappointed place

at the right hand of the Father.

Be not troubled, says Marcus Aurelius, *for in a little while
you will be no one and nowhere.*

We must continue to exit. To exist.
We must
continue at once to exit and exist.

Fugit, Time.
I would be
disconnected, for a while, from the server Kronos:
No One, No-
where; self-culling; de-verbed; averbal.

But dailiness
clings to everything, *God from god,* un-
scrub-off-able, like algae
to the lawn table's iron underslats.
I took a toothbrush to it, its bristles all gone green.

Everything
today feels *nounal,* stuck
in its own thingy
timefulness

like driblets
of rain each surface struggles
not to let slip again away.

Agnus Dei

Out of the ordinary something keeps
busting loose to seek
asylum in "Nonordinary
reality," like the "soul parts"
the shamanist's pamphlet assures me
have gone missing, lopped
off one by one through loss, or grief, or trauma, like
the leg of an amoeba. "When a soul part leaves
it can't come back on its own," but needs
professional intervention:
ALL SOUL PARTS RETURNED
goes the moneyback guarantee.

I can feel, some days, their going:
the tear of them, the ripped
and bruised lesion where they split.

If any of these symptoms apply,
says the pamphlet,
part of your soul is seriously considering leaving
right now:
feeling unappreciated (check);
feeling no matter what you do, your
efforts are thwarted (check).

Soul loss is imminent. Get help at once.

I give the computer my email login and password:
BAD REQUEST it says.
I double click on Google News, for word
of the Batman Massacre: BAD REQUEST.
Every inquiry, this summer, gets turned

back, question and answer dissevered like
rebel and dutiful soul-parts.
Get help at once. Who made us? Bad request.
Why did God make us? Bad request.
If God is everywhere, then why do we not see Him? Bad request.
Strongly or mildly agree, or disagree:
I don't have a particular sense of meaning
and purpose in my life: Bad, Bad Request.
I feel able to take anything on:
Sundry
soul parts are currently
incommunicado. I do not feel
able at this time
to take this question and its
psychospiritual implications
on.

A "mass noun" means a substance
abstract and 'indefinitely divisible,' that can't
rightly be used in the plural, or with
the indefinite article:

Some *the*s became indefinite, and plural.
The happinesses lost their soul parts
and went wandering. Get
a help at once.

Mass is "a collection
of incoherent parts
regarded as forming one body." Minute
by minute I go strafing
out of and right
smack back into the middle

of the Ordinary
of the Mass. Agnus Dei, Lamb
of God. Who takest away.
Who takest away? Who takest away?

Come now, World-to-Come, things seem so
here:
so thick with *now* and *noun*.
Ora means *hour*, means *now*, means *pray*:
Ora pro nobis. Pray for now. Pray for *us* now
and at the hour

when now shall be no more.

BENEDICTUS

Just
thing on thing, Kronos
with its beget beget beget
and consume
what's been begotten—

Time's pointless By Enlarge:
Weedwhack, *Deadwood, Hair Loss
Answers, What Would Jesus
Deconstruct.*

The 0 right smack in the middle:

If nothing matters, says Thomas Nagel, the fact
that nothing matters

can't matter either.
Why haven't I found myself

consoled by that?

Let today mark the Mortification
part of the Order of Salvation, this
panicsense that nothing that happens signifies, nothing counts, and nothing
means—

Dona nobis pacem. Keep a tight asshole,
my father-in-law likes to say.
Meaning: Watch, wait.

In good time even this
Mortification
will matter; will count; take
its place inside the gradual
ordinals of our redeeming.

———————————

Bene-
diction: spoken-
well, as if
we could utter the Ordinary of our prayers
until our saying made the things we spoke of

well.

———————————

My friend's daughter
Lily got so happy on a camping trip she burst
out, *Oh, I wish I were here.*
That's Lily's Subjunctive
Paradox: sate
and still want. Synchronous sate and want.

———————————

It's not enough to be WANTED,
growled a bodiless brogue in a dream,
You've got to be GREATLY TAKEN.

Look for me then
in the ellipsis, self-
tripler of the period,
what meant to make a hard stop

but goes on. I'm here, with
some of my soul parts

greatly taken.

———————————

Thy will be done, Lord, we pray, as if
it weren't.
Somebody's got to want things
not to be

otherwise; otherwise
how can we be
particularly pleased,
wishing we
were here just where and as and right
smack in the middle of
what and why we are?

Gloria

We *look for*
the Resurrection of the Dead, and the Life of the World To Come.
We look, and we look.
We look for the *exit*
in the *ressurexit*
mortuorum:

we *must*, we think, continue to exist.

Be comforted, No One, Nowhere:
the pneuma will stay shut inside your eyes,
inside what sockets you have left, and bring you
no sad tidings.
The skin has left the palms
of all who ever
clapped for you.

Something mergent to say, Jin would announce, when he was three,
whenever he wanted to interrupt.

Merge emergency urgent.

This summer has something mergent to say, *in nomine domini.*
Glory be to what contrived

ears to hear it.

I can't find the word *Conditions* in the Glossary; how
unconditional, then, will be Your grace?

———————————————

If my Perseverent Belief in Staying Saved
happens before my Election
to *be* saved, is
my Order of Salvation still OK?

———————————————

If I can agree that the world is a *good* place,
by how many points will that raise my Happiness score?

If desire could be untwisted
like an iron coil
so we want
what is and not
what's not.

———————————————

I do not think the world is a good place.
I moderately disagree.
I do not think the world is a good place.

Deum de Deo. Deum de Deo.
Deum verum et Deo vero.
Outbreath. Inbreath. Pneuma's inward-nesting.
Soul parts split, regather.

I do not think. The world is a good place.

NONORDINARY TO THE POEMS

PART I: *THOU MUST LEAVE*

Report to the Provost on the Progress of My Leave: This poem is possessed by Shakespeare's Sonnet 73, "That time of year thou mayst in me behold," phrases and words of which recur throughout.

Reading Jesus Again, with a New Prescription: Ricky Alan Mayotte's *The Complete Jesus: All the Sayings of Jesus Gathered in a Single Volume for the First Time* (Steerforth, 1998) collects the sayings attributed to Christ by twenty-four ancient sources, including New Testament texts and apocryphal and Gnostic writings.

Neuroparousial: "Parousia," in Christian theology, refers to the second coming of Christ.

PART II: *DISORIENTATION PSALM*

Disorientation Psalm: Tohu Bohu—: Arthur Schopenhauer (1788–1860), the German philosopher said to be the most pessimistic thinker in the history of human thought. Schopenhauer raised to a higher power Job's curse of the day he was born: Schopenhauer repeatedly, over the course of his thousands of pages of prose, cursing the fact that the *universe* itself exists.

Central to Schopenhauer's thinking is his concept of The Will: "Will is the thing-in-itself, the inner content, the essence of the world. Life, the visible world, the phenomenon, is only the mirror of the will. Therefore life accompanies the will as inseparably as the shadow accompanies the body" (*The World as Will and Representation*, vol. 2, Book 4). The Will represents a continuous and purposeless striving inherent in the nature of all things: "The existence of the plant is just such a restless, never satisfied striving, a ceaseless tendency through ever-ascending forms, till the end, the seed, becomes a new starting-point; and this repeated *ad infinitum*—nowhere an end, nowhere a final satisfaction, nowhere a resting-place . . . if there is no final end of striving, there is no measure and end of suffering . . . this appears to us much more distinctly when we consider the nature of brutes and man. Willing and striving is its whole being . . . But the basis of all willing is need, deficiency, and thus pain. Consequently, the nature of brutes and man is subject to pain originally and through its very being."

"Psalm of Disorientation": Walter Brueggeman, in *Spirituality of the Psalms* and other books, divides the psalms into Psalms of Orientation, which declare faith and a sense of being-at-home in the world; the Psalms of Disorientation, which give voice to a deep sense of disillusion with the promises of the covenant and the cosmos; and the Psalms of Reorientation, which work through the doubts and dreads voiced with such anguish in the latter. The psalms of disorientation, Brueggeman writes, "lead us into dangerous acknowledgement of how life really is . . . They cause us to think unthinkable thoughts and utter unutterable words" (*Spirituality of the Psalms*).

"Fiat lux" and "tohu bohu": Fiat lux, the Latin for God's first words in Genesis—"Let there be light." "Tohu bohu": from the Hebrew of the second verse of Genesis, variously translated as the primordial earth having been "without form, and void," "formless and empty," "a formless void," "waste and empty," "without shape or form." As one translation puts it bluntly: "The earth didn't have any shape. And it was empty."

Disorientation Psalm: Looking Down the Cliff, with Schopenhauer, on Black Friday: The so-called Fiscal Cliff on January 1, 2013 was a potential massive series of slashes to federal spending and enormous tax increases resulting from expiration of the Bush era tax cuts, combined with across-the-board spending cuts resulting from the failure of a congressional budget commission to agree on principles of deficit reduction. Economists and politicians warned of economic calamity unless something was done to steer away from that cliff. Congress passed a last-minute compromise on January 1 to delay the Fiscal Cliff while avoiding the larger issues of federal debt and deficit spending.

Reading The Purpose-Driven Life, *with Schopenhauer:* Hugh S. Moorehead wrote to dozens of famous thinkers, artists, philosophers, and writers, asking them to comment on a postcard on their thoughts on the meaning of life. He published the results in *The Meaning of Life* (1988). The epigraph is Jung's answer.

"There's been another massacre": there have been so many more since, it may already be necessary to footnote: on December 14, 2012, in the second largest mass-shooting in American history, Adam Lanza murdered his mother and then shot twenty young children and six adults to death at Sandy Hook Elementary School in Newtown, Connecticut, before committing suicide.

Like Ezekiel: In Ezekiel 37, God commands Ezekiel to prophesy before a valley of dry bones: "and as I prophesied, there was a noise, and behold a shaking, and the bones came together, bone to his bone. And when I beheld, lo, the sinews and the flesh came up upon them, and the skin covered them above: but there was no breath in them. Then said he unto me, Prophesy unto the wind, prophesy, son of man, and say to the wind, Thus saith the Lord God; COME FROM THE FOUR WINDS, O BREATH, AND BREATHE UPON THESE SLAIN, THAT THEY MAY LIVE. SO I PROPHESIED AS HE COMMANDED ME, AND THE BREATH CAME INTO THEM, AND THEY LIVED, AND STOOD UP UPON THEIR FEET, AN EXCEEDING GREAT ARMY."

PART III: *HYMENEAL*

Antithalamion: Opposite of a "pro"-thalamion, a term invented by Spenser for a poem celebrating a marriage (meaning, in his case, "before the wedding bed.")

What Do You Think the Poet Is Trying to Say?: to "denature," in biochemistry, is to "treat (a protein or the like) by chemical or physical means so as to alter its original state."

Offspring Insprung: Cleromancy is the art of divination through casting lots or dice.

Intra tua vulnera absconde me: from the Medieval Latin prayer "Anima Christi," "Within thy wounds hide me."

PART IV: *THE SIXTH DUST*

Cleft for Me Let Me Hide Myself from Thee: Reverend Augustus Montague Toplady is said to have composed the lyrics to the hymn "Rock of Ages" ("Rock of ages, cleft for me/Let me hide myself in Thee . . .") while taking shelter from a storm in a rock gorge in England. In Exodus 33, Yahweh says to Moses: "Thou canst not see my face: for there shall no man see me, and live . . . Behold, there is a place by me, and thou shalt stand upon a rock: And it shall come to pass, while my glory passeth by, that I will put thee in a cleft of the rock, and will cover thee with my hand while I pass by: And I will take away mine hand, and thou shalt see my back parts: but my face shall not be seen."

Paraclete, or Comforter, one-called-to-help, is a name for the Holy Spirit.

Zeno's arrow: one of the ancient Greek philosopher's famous paradoxes of motion. The arrow, according to the paradox, cannot move, because it cannot be in two places at once; when it is where it is it cannot be where it is not, so can never arrive. Another of Zeno's paradoxes claims that because anything in motion travels halfway to its destination, then half of the remaining distance, then half of the distance remaining after that, etc. nothing can reach its destination, as the distance is forever halvable.

Pascal: "What else does this craving, and this helplessness, proclaim but that there was once in man a true happiness, of which all that now remains is the empty print and trace? This he tries in vain to fill with everything around him, seeking in things that are not there the help he cannot find in those that are, though none can help, since this infinite abyss can be filled only with an infinite and unchangeable object; in other words by God himself." (*Pensees* 10.148)

———————————

Such and Such and Such and Such:

Sunyata (the Sanskrit word usually translated as *emptiness)* is defined by the Oxford English Dictionary as "the concept of the essential emptiness of all things and of ultimate reality as a void beyond phenomena." Masao Abe, in *Zen and Western Thought,* writes that "when ignorance is realized for what it is through the realization of no-self, one may awaken to suchness, in which everything is recognized in its uniqueness and particularity . . . the realization of suchness is the positive aspect of the realization of Emptiness."

The Buddha is said to have said, "It is not the idea of emptiness that makes things empty; rather they are simply empty. It is not the idea of the absence of any ultimate cause that makes things lack such a cause; rather they simply lack an ultimate cause. It is not the idea of the absence of an ultimate purpose that makes things lack an ultimate purpose: rather they simply lack an ultimate purpose . . . emptiness is the exhaustion of all philosophical views. I call incurable whoever holds emptiness as a philosophical view."

Seventy Verses on Emptiness: Treatise by second century C.E. Indian Buddhist philosopher Nagarjuna, *Sunyatasaptati.*

Haecceitas: Duns Scotus' term for quiddity or "thisness," the quality that distinguishes a thing and makes it exactly what it is.

PART V: *THE MASS OF THE ORDINARY*
Kyrie—"Christ at the fig tree": The parable of the fig tree in Luke 13: "He spake also this parable; A certain man had a fig tree planted in his vineyard; and he came and sought fruit thereon, and found none. Then said he unto the dresser of his vineyard, Behold, these three years I come seeking fruit on this fig tree, and find none: cut it down; why cumbereth it the ground? And he answering said unto him,

Lord, let it alone this year also, till I shall dig about it, and dung it: And if it bear fruit, well: and if not, then after that thou shalt cut it down."

"Oxford Happiness" Questionnaire was developed by psychologists at Oxford to provide a quick numerical score of a patient's current level of happiness. The questionnaire asks takers to choose an option from slightly to strongly agree or slightly to strongly disagree with each of twenty-nine statements, some of which are incorporated into the language of "The Mass of the Ordinary" throughout.

Embolism—Embolism (meaning, etymologically, to interject or interpose) is the name of the prayer during Mass that elaborates on the last verse of the Our Father. Part of the text of the Embolism appears as the epigraph of this poem.

Galen: Greek physician and philosopher of the second century, C.E., one of the most influential thinkers in the history of ancient medicine.

Epictetus: Greek Stoic philosopher of the first and second century C.E.

Sanctus—*Celaenia excavate* of Australia and other spiders have evolved the camouflage of uncanny resemblance to excrement, which both protects them from predators like birds and allows them to prey on butterflies and other creatures that are attracted to the excrement of birds the spiders so resemble. "Wont to settle on these evacuations" is from a description of such a spider in Jean Massart and Emile Vandervelde's 1895 book *Parasitism: Organic and Social* : on the strength of "its extraordinary resemblance to the droppings of a bird" the spider is "able to seize the butterflies which are wont to settle on these evacuations."

In the Mass the Sanctus immediately precedes the rite of the Eucharist, in which bread and wine camouflage the body and blood of Christ.

Fraction Rite: the words of the Ordinary of the Mass ("God from God, light from light, true god from true god, one in being with the Father; through Him all things are made, for us men and for our salvation He came down from heaven") move through this and other sections of "The Mass of the Ordinary."

Kronos or Cronus: Titan god of time and father of Zeus, who famously ate all of his offspring except Zeus, who managed to escape when Rhea fed Kronos a stone wrapped in swaddling clothes instead.

Agnus Dei: The words of the Catholic liturgy—"Lamb of God, who taketh away the sins of the world, have mercy on us; Lamb of God, who taketh away the sins of the world, have mercy on us; Lamb of God, who taketh away the sins of the world, grant us peace"—move through this poem.

Batman Massacre: On July 20, 2012, in Aurora, Colorado, a gunman entered a movie theater during a midnight showing of *The Dark Night Rises,* murdering twelve people and injuring seventy others.

The questions in the second section—Who made us? Why did God make us? If God is everywhere, then why do we not see Him?—are from the Baltimore Catechism.

Ora pro nobis: Latin, pray for us. In the Rosary prayer: "Holy Mary, mother of God, pray for us sinners now and at the hour of our death; pray for us now and at the hour of our death."

Ora means, in addition to *pray* in Latin, *hour* or *now* in Italian.

Benedictus: Thomas Nagel, "The Absurd" (in his *Mortal Questions,* Cambridge University Press, 1979)

Order of Salvation (Latin, *ordo salutis*): the sequential series of steps, in Christian theology, leading to salvation: including such stages as Faith, Contrition, Regeneration, Purgation, and Theosis (taking on the divine nature).

Gloria: In the Catholic Mass' ordinary: "We look for the Resurrection of the Dead, and the life of the world to come."

Resurrexit mortuorem: Latin, the resurrection of the dead

In nomine Domine: Latin, in the name of the Lord

ACKNOWLEDGMENTS

Enormous thanks to the editors of the following journals where these poems originally appeared:

Cincinnati Review: "On Marriage";
Crazyhorse: "What Do You Think the Poet Is Trying to Say?";
Denver Quarterly: "Offspring Insprung";
FIELD: "Antithalamion," "The Mass of the Ordinary: Kyrie," "The Mass of the Ordinary: Fraction Rite," "Report to the Provost on the Progress of My Leave," "Revised Catechism";
The Georgia Review: "Disorientation Psalm: Reading *The Purpose Driven Life*, with Schopenhauer";
Gettysburg Review: "Such and Such and Such and Such," "Nuptial Song" (as "Lyrebird"); "Reading Jesus Again, with a New Prescription";
Hotel Amerika: "Disorientation Psalm: The Last Good" (as "Last Praisesong for Arthur Schopenhauer");
Image: "Cleft for Me Let Me Hide Myself from Thee";
Kenyon Review: "Me Meaneth," "The Name of the Island Was Marriage," "The Mass of the Ordinary: Embolism," "The Mass of the Ordinary: Agnus Dei";
Poetry Northwest: "Disorientation Psalm: Tohu Bohu," "Disorientation Psalm: 'I Don't Like My Soul Parts'";
Terminus: "The Mass of the Ordinary: Credo," "The Mass of the Ordinary: Sanctus."

"The Name of the Island Was Marriage" was reprinted on *Poetry Daily* (www.poems.com). "The Mass of the Ordinary: Credo" was reprinted in *The Orison Anthology* (Orison Press, 2016).

Enormous thanks to friends and colleagues who read many drafts of these poems and this book: Timothy Liu, Luke Hankins, Bill Wenthe, Dan Tobin, Chris Patton; and to Thor Hansen, who brought me the ALL SOUL PARTS RETURNED pamphlet and told me I needed to get some soul parts back; to Bruce Beasley the sculptor, for his astonishing work and for *Offspring*; and to Peter Conners, Jenna Fisher, Ron Martin-Dent, Kelly Hatton, and everybody else at BOA: working with you has been a complete delight.

The cover art on this book incorporates "spirit writing" from J.B. Murray (1908–88), a self-taught artist from Glascock County, Georgia. An illiterate African-American sharecropper, Murray experienced a religious vision at the age of seventy while watering his potato patch and began painting for the first time. Many of the one thousand paintings he completed in his last decade of life incorporate a script he believed was the inspired writing of the Holy Spirit, and which he interpreted by reading it through a jar of water from his well.

About the Author

Bruce Beasley is a professor of English at Western Washington University in Bellingham. He is the author of seven previous collections of poems, including *Theophobia* (BOA Editions, 2012). His previous books won the Ohio State University Press/*The Journal* Award (for *The Creation,* 1993), the Colorado Prize for Poetry (selected by Charles Wright, 1996), and the University of Georgia Press Contemporary Poetry Series Award (for *Lord Brain*, 2005). Beasley has won fellowships from the National Endowment for the Arts and the Artist Trust of Washington and three Pushcart Prizes in poetry. His work appears in such journals as *Kenyon Review, Georgia Review, Field, Image,* and *Gettysburg Review.*

BOA Editions, Ltd., American Poets Continuum Series

No. 1 *The Fuhrer Bunker: A Cycle of Poems in Progress*
W. D. Snodgrass

No. 2 *She*
M. L. Rosenthal

No. 3 *Living With Distance*
Ralph J. Mills, Jr.

No. 4 *Not Just Any Death*
Michael Waters

No. 5 *That Was Then: New and Selected Poems*
Isabella Gardner

No. 6 *Things That Happen Where There Aren't Any People*
William Stafford

No. 7 *The Bridge of Change: Poems 1974–1980*
John Logan

No. 8 *Signatures*
Joseph Stroud

No. 9 *People Live Here: Selected Poems 1949–1983*
Louis Simpson

No. 10 *Yin*
Carolyn Kizer

No. 11 *Duhamel: Ideas of Order in Little Canada*
Bill Tremblay

No. 12 *Seeing It Was So*
Anthony Piccione

No. 13 *Hyam Plutzik: The Collected Poems*

No. 14 *Good Woman: Poems and a Memoir 1969–1980*
Lucille Clifton

No. 15 *Next: New Poems*
Lucille Clifton

No. 16 *Roxa: Voices of the Culver Family*
William B. Patrick

No. 17 *John Logan: The Collected Poems*

No. 18 *Isabella Gardner: The Collected Poems*

No. 19 *The Sunken Lightship*
Peter Makuck

No. 20 *The City in Which I Love You*
Li-Young Lee

No. 21 *Quilting: Poems 1987–1990*
Lucille Clifton

No. 22 *John Logan: The Collected Fiction*

No. 23 *Shenandoah and Other Verse Plays*
Delmore Schwartz

No. 24 *Nobody Lives on Arthur Godfrey Boulevard*
Gerald Costanzo

No. 25 *The Book of Names: New and Selected Poems*
Barton Sutter

No. 26 *Each in His Season*
W. D. Snodgrass

No. 27 *Wordworks: Poems Selected and New*
Richard Kostelanetz

No. 28 *What We Carry*
Dorianne Laux

No. 29 *Red Suitcase*
Naomi Shihab Nye

No. 30 *Song*
Brigit Pegeen Kelly

No. 31 *The Fuehrer Bunker: The Complete Cycle*
W. D. Snodgrass

No. 32 *For the Kingdom*
Anthony Piccione

No. 33 *The Quicken Tree*
Bill Knott

No. 34 *These Upraised Hands*
William B. Patrick

No. 35 *Crazy Horse in Stillness*
William Heyen

No. 36 *Quick, Now, Always*
Mark Irwin

No. 37 *I Have Tasted the Apple*
Mary Crow

No. 38 *The Terrible Stories*
Lucille Clifton

No. 39 *The Heat of Arrivals*
Ray Gonzalez

No. 40 *Jimmy & Rita*
Kim Addonizio

No. 41 *Green Ash, Red Maple, Black Gum*
Michael Waters

No. 42 *Against Distance*
Peter Makuck

No. 43 *The Night Path*
Laurie Kutchins

No. 44 *Radiography*
Bruce Bond

No. 45 *At My Ease: Uncollected Poems of the Fifties and Sixties*
David Ignatow

No. 46 *Trillium*
Richard Foerster

No. 47 *Fuel*
Naomi Shihab Nye

No. 48 *Gratitude*
Sam Hamill

No. 49 *Diana, Charles, & the Queen*
William Heyen

No. 50 *Plus Shipping*
Bob Hicok

No. 51 *Cabato Sentora*
Ray Gonzalez

No. 52 *We Didn't Come Here for This*
William B. Patrick

No. 53 *The Vandals*
Alan Michael Parker

No. 54 *To Get Here*
Wendy Mnookin

No. 55 *Living Is What I Wanted: Last Poems*
David Ignatow

No. 56 *Dusty Angel*
Michael Blumenthal

No. 57 *The Tiger Iris*
Joan Swift

No. 58 *White City*
Mark Irwin

No. 59 *Laugh at the End of the World: Collected Comic Poems 1969–1999*
Bill Knott

No. 60 *Blessing the Boats: New and Selected Poems: 1988–2000*
Lucille Clifton

No. 61 *Tell Me*
Kim Addonizio

No. 62 *Smoke*
Dorianne Laux

No. 63 *Parthenopi: New and Selected Poems*
Michael Waters

No. 64 *Rancho Notorious*
Richard Garcia

No. 65 *Jam*
Joe-Anne McLaughlin

No. 66 *A. Poulin, Jr. Selected Poems*
Edited, with an Introduction by Michael Waters

No. 67 *Small Gods of Grief*
Laure-Anne Bosselaar

No. 68 *Book of My Nights*
Li-Young Lee

No. 69 *Tulip Farms and Leper Colonies*
Charles Harper Webb

No. 70 *Double Going*
Richard Foerster

No. 71 *What He Took*
Wendy Mnookin

No. 72 *The Hawk Temple at Tierra Grande*
Ray Gonzalez

No. 73 *Mules of Love*
Ellen Bass

No. 74 *The Guests at the Gate*
Anthony Piccione

No. 75 *Dumb Luck*
Sam Hamill

No. 76 *Love Song with Motor Vehicles*
Alan Michael Parker

No. 77 *Life Watch*
Willis Barnstone

No. 78 *The Owner of the House: New Collected Poems 1940–2001*
Louis Simpson

No. 79 *Is*
Wayne Dodd

No. 80 *Late*
Cecilia Woloch

No. 81 *Precipitates*
Debra Kang Dean

No. 82 *The Orchard*
Brigit Pegeen Kelly

No. 83 *Bright Hunger*
Mark Irwin

No. 84 *Desire Lines: New and Selected Poems*
Lola Haskins

No. 85 *Curious Conduct*
Jeanne Marie Beaumont

No. 86 *Mercy*
Lucille Clifton

No. 87 *Model Homes*
Wayne Koestenbaum

No. 88 *Farewell to the Starlight in Whiskey*
Barton Sutter

No. 89 *Angels for the Burning*
David Mura

No. 90 *The Rooster's Wife*
Russell Edson

No. 91 *American Children*
Jim Simmerman

No. 92 *Postcards from the Interior*
Wyn Cooper

No. 93 *You & Yours*
Naomi Shihab Nye

No. 94 *Consideration of the Guitar: New and Selected Poems 1986–2005*
Ray Gonzalez

No. 95 *Off-Season in the Promised Land*
Peter Makuck

No. 96 *The Hoopoe's Crown*
Jacqueline Osherow

No. 97 *Not for Specialists: New and Selected Poems*
W. D. Snodgrass

No. 98 *Splendor*
Steve Kronen

No. 99 *Woman Crossing a Field*
Deena Linett

No. 100 *The Burning of Troy*
Richard Foerster

No. 101 *Darling Vulgarity*
Michael Waters

No. 102 *The Persistence of Objects*
Richard Garcia

No. 103 *Slope of the Child Everlasting*
Laurie Kutchins

No. 104 *Broken Hallelujahs*
Sean Thomas Dougherty

No. 105 *Peeping Tom's Cabin: Comic Verse 1928–2008*
X. J. Kennedy

No. 106 *Disclamor*
G.C. Waldrep

No. 107 *Encouragement for a Man Falling to His Death*
Christopher Kennedy

No. 108 *Sleeping with Houdini*
Nin Andrews

No. 109 *Nomina*
Karen Volkman

No. 110 *The Fortieth Day*
Kazim Ali

No. 111 *Elephants & Butterflies*
Alan Michael Parker

No. 112 *Voices*
Lucille Clifton

No. 113 *The Moon Makes Its Own Plea*
Wendy Mnookin

No. 114 *The Heaven-Sent Leaf*
Katy Lederer

No. 115 *Struggling Times*
Louis Simpson

No. 116 *And*
Michael Blumenthal

No. 117 *Carpathia*
Cecilia Woloch

No. 118 *Seasons of Lotus, Seasons of Bone*
Matthew Shenoda

No. 119 *Sharp Stars*
Sharon Bryan

No. 120 *Cool Auditor*
Ray Gonzalez

No. 121 *Long Lens: New and Selected Poems*
Peter Makuck

No. 122 *Chaos Is the New Calm*
Wyn Cooper

No. 123 *Diwata*
Barbara Jane Reyes

No. 124 *Burning of the Three Fires*
Jeanne Marie Beaumont

No. 125 *Sasha Sings the Laundry on the Line*
Sean Thomas Dougherty

No. 126 *Your Father on the Train of Ghosts*
G.C. Waldrep and John Gallaher

No. 127 *Ennui Prophet*
Christopher Kennedy

No. 128 *Transfer*
Naomi Shihab Nye

No. 129 *Gospel Night*
Michael Waters

No. 130 *The Hands of Strangers: Poems from the Nursing Home*
Janice N. Harrington

No. 131 *Kingdom Animalia*
Aracelis Girmay

No. 132 *True Faith*
Ira Sadoff

No. 133 *The Reindeer Camps and Other Poems*
Barton Sutter

No. 134 *The Collected Poems of Lucille Clifton: 1965–2010*

No. 135 *To Keep Love Blurry*
Craig Morgan Teicher

No. 136 *Theophobia*
Bruce Beasley

No. 137 *Refuge*
Adrie Kusserow

No. 138 *The Book of Goodbyes*
Jillian Weise

No. 139 *Birth Marks*
Jim Daniels

No. 140 *No Need of Sympathy*
Fleda Brown

No. 141 *There's a Box in the Garage You Can Beat with a Stick*
Michael Teig

No. 142 *The Keys to the Jail*
Keetje Kuipers

No. 143 *All You Ask for Is Longing: New and Selected Poems 1994–2014*
Sean Thomas Dougherty

No. 144 *Copia*
Erika Meitner

No. 145 *The Chair: Prose Poems*
Richard Garcia

No. 146 *In a Landscape*
John Gallaher

No. 147 *Fanny Says*
Nickole Brown

No. 148 *Why God Is a Woman*
Nin Andrews

No. 149 *Testament*
G.C. Waldrep

No. 150 *I'm No Longer Troubled by the Extravagance*
Rick Bursky

No. 151 *Antidote for Night*
Marsha de la O

No. 152 *Beautiful Wall*
Ray Gonzalez

No. 153 *the black maria*
Aracelis Girmay

No. 154 *Celestial Joyride*
Michael Waters

No. 155 *Whereso*
Karen Volkman

No. 156 *The Day's Last Light Reddens the Leaves of the Copper Beech*
Stephen Dobyns

No. 157 *The End of Pink*
Kathryn Nuernberger

No. 158 *Mandatory Evacuation*
Peter Makuck

No. 159 *Primitive: The Art and Life of Horace H. Pippin*
Janice N. Harrington

No. 160 *The Trembling Answers*
Craig Morgan Teicher

No. 161 *Bye-Bye Land*
Christian Barter

No. 162 *Sky Country*
Christine Kitano

No. 163 *All Soul Parts Returned*
Bruce Beasley

COLOPHON

BOA Editions, Ltd., a not-for-profit publisher of poetry and other literary works, fosters readership and appreciation of contemporary literature. By identifying, cultivating, and publishing both new and established poets and selecting authors of unique literary talent, BOA brings high-quality literature to the public. Support for this effort comes from the sale of its publications, grant funding, and private donations.

The publication of this book is made possible, in part,
by the support of the following individuals:

Anonymous x 3
Gwen & Gary Conners
Gouvernet Arts Fund
Peg Heminway, *in honor of Grant Holcomb*
Sandi Henschel
Christopher Kennedy
X. J. & Dorothy M. Kennedy
Laurie Kutchins
Ron & Melanie Martin-Dent, *in honor of our son*
Boo Poulin
Deborah Ronnen & Sherman Levey
Steven O. Russell & Phyllis Rifkin-Russell
Sue Stewart, *in memory of Stephen L. Raymond*
Michael Waters & Mihaela Moscaliuc
Bernadette Weaver-Catalana

Printed in the USA
CPSIA information can be obtained
at www.ICGtesting.com
JSHW052018140824
68134JS00027B/2544

9 781942 683452

POETRY / RELIGION

When the Gnostic Gospels collide with new age spiritualism, the Oxford Happiness Test, and treatises on Buddhist practice, we know we are in the territory of a Bruce Beasley collection. Alternately devout and heretical, Beasley—known for his intense and continuing soul-quest through previous award-winning books—interrogates the absurdities, psychic violence, and spiritual condition of 21st-century America with despair, philosophic intelligence, and piercing humor.

———

"All *Soul Parts Returned* is a dynamic catechism-in-progress, laden with prayers, addresses, and meditations on God's 'pouring-apart of opposites.' Bruce Beasley reminds us that to come apart or 'go missing' is not necessarily to be lost, and his lyrics struggle movingly with limitation and loss, with familial bonds and inheritance, and with the way we can neither fully hide in nor emerge from our vocabularies. The prismatic language of these poems shimmers with a love of 'the inchoation of words': 'Out of the ordinary something keeps/ busting loose…' These poems gather, return, and enlarge it."

—MARY SZYBIST, WINNER OF THE 2013 NATIONAL BOOK AWARD FOR POETRY

BOA
EDITIONS LTD
250 N. GOODMAN ST.
SUITE 306
ROCHESTER, NY 14607
WWW.BOAEDITIONS.ORG

ISBN 978-1-942683-45-2

90000

9 781942 683452

COVER ART:
J. B. Murray courtesy of
the Estate of J. B. Murray

AUTHOR PHOTO:
Jin Beasley

COVER DESIGN
Sandy Knight